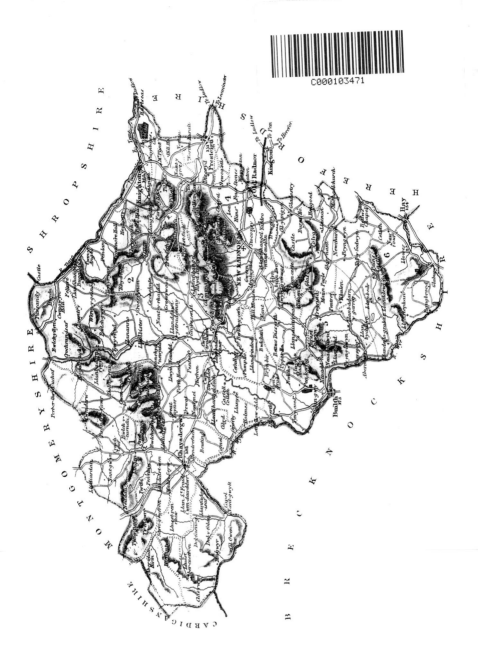

THE FOUR GRACES
AND OTHER PRAYERS TO
CELEBRATE RADNOR 2014 AD

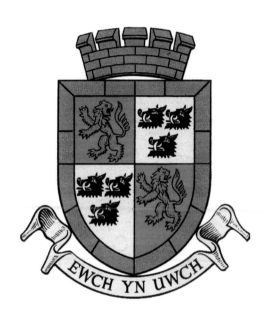

EWCH YN UWCH

THE FOUR GRACES
AND OTHER PRAYERS TO
CELEBRATE RADNOR 2014 AD

TEXT SELECTED BY
PENELOPE BOURDILLON

ILLUSTRATIONS OF THE CHURCHES IN RADNORSHIRE BY
MARCIA GIBSON-WATT

First edition published by Bluestone Books 2000

Second Edition Published by Greyhound Self-Publishing 2013
Malvern, Worcestershire, United Kingdom.

Printed and bound by Aspect Design
89 Newtown Road, Malvern, Worcs. WR14 1PD
United Kingdom
Tel: 01684 561567
E-mail: allan@aspect-design.net
Website: www.aspect-design.net

A copy of this book has been deposited with the British Library Board

Extracts from the Authorised Version of the Bible (The King James
Bible), the rights in which are vested in the Crown, are reproduced by
permission of the Crown's Patentee, Cambridge University Press.

The artwork used on the original bookmark for *The Four Graces* has
now been used as the front cover for this edition.

ISBN 978-1-909219-14-4

Also by Penelope Bourdillon and Marcia Gibson-Watt:
A.C.T.S. 1
Hope in the Valley

And by Penelope Bourdillon:
How God Can Peel an Onion

DEDICATION

TO THE PEOPLE OF RADNOR

How lovely is your dwelling place,
O God Thou Lord of Hosts!
My soul has a desire and longing
to enter the courts of the Lord.
Psalm 84:1

THE CHURCH IS THE BRIDE OF CHRIST

CONTENTS

PART II

Thoughts on Living

*'There should be in the soul halls of space, avenues of leisure
and porticoes of silence where God walks.'*
Jeremy Taylor, seventeenth century Anglican Divine

Part III

The Bible and Prayer

Ask God to remove barriers
and change attitudes where necessary

Part IV
Death, Suffering, Healing and Light – Always Light
'The fear of the Lord is the beginning of wisdom.'

FOREWORD TO THE FIRST EDITION

As a native of Pantydwr and Chairman of the Council of The Royal Welsh Agricultural Society, it gives me the greatest pleasure to write a foreword to this publication in the Millennium year, when Radnorshire is our Host County.

For those who live in the area the book will be of special significance. For many, the churches depicted will be their family place of worship. Everyone, wherever they live, will appreciate the art and derive comfort and benefit from the prayers that accompany the paintings.

I have always believed that, to enjoy a full and happy life, one needs to cultivate an equilibrium between the material, the aesthetic and the spiritual aspects. This book will help us to achieve this.

I congratulate Marcia Gibson-Watt for giving of her time and using her talent in such a constructive way and Penelope Bourdillon for enhancing the paintings with her thoughtful selection of prayers and readings.

We can browse and contemplate, in our reflective hours, this compilation of their work and perhaps, in our leisure time, visit and imbibe the aura of some of the sixty-three churches depicted.

It is a book for us, and for the generations that follow us, to treasure and to enjoy.

Meuric Rees

Meuric Rees CBE FRAgS

St Tecla's, Llandegley

Foreword to Second Edition

As another native of Pantydwr it gives me much pleasure to endorse all that our good friend Meuric has written on the previous page.

It was very exciting to see this wonderful book come to life for Radnor's Feature Year in 2000 and I'm sure that its re-run will be equally well received.

Over the last decade I have heard of many people turning to this book, sometimes just for their own pleasure, but sometimes to succour them during particularly difficult times in their lives.

In the Millennium Edition, Llandegley, the church I have attended since I married, takes pride of place on the front cover and with the sheep in the foreground it encapsulates country life and the importance of worship and fellowship in our local communities.

St Garmon's at St Harmon, the church I attended as a child, paints a similar scene of rural life.

I trust that the Four Graces will now reach a whole new generation and that they too will treasure it.

Rhian Duggan

Rhian Duggan
President of the Royal Welsh Show for Radnor 2014

St Cynllo's, Nantmel

Part I

Countryside, Nature and Love

The First Grace

Grant we remember, Lord divine,
These gifts of food and drink are thine.
Your bounty gives us all we eat,
The crops we grow, the rich Welsh meat.
You bless us with those caring hands
Which farm our farms and tend our lands.
Protect our farmers from distress,
Be slow to chide and swift to bless.
O Lord, we praise you as we ought
For rural beauty, country sport;
And for community, the way
We celebrate it here today.
Pour favour on our lunch, our show,
That home we may rejoicing go.
Through Jesus Christ, our Lord.
Amen

The Reverend Morgan Llewellyn

*The mountains skipped like rams,
and the little hills like lambs.*
Psalm 114:4

St Padarn's, Llanbadarn-y-Garreg

Babell – The Chapel

Babell! Empty and bare!
Come back with me there!
A lonely hare rises from the nettles,
And scuttles from the surrounds of Babell.
From the nettles . . . that are the substitute for flowers
On the graves of people.
Succour to the succumb of a valley . . .

Where people worshipped in days of old,
And worshipped God instead of Gold.
With copper heavy on the plate.
Collective Love! That was the rate
For Godly loving, and hating hate!
Where Preachers preached their Gospels of fire!
Today . . . Empty: enclosed with wire.

O fryniau Caersalem was sung with a tear,
Praise ye the Lord . . . with gusto and fear,
The children loved their Ysgol Sul,[1]
And learned to tread the llwybr cul.[2]
They sang 'bout Jesus mild and meek,
They sang it seven days a week.
At school . . . while playing . . . and at home,
They sang it together, they sang it alone!

Where long ago, new born babes were christened,
And oaths of matrimony chronicled
In front of you . . . Dear Lord of Grace!
Forgive us Welsh this Holy disgrace.
For Babell gwympa er ei chryfed,
O Lord forgive us all our dyled![3]
Forgive us that we closed the door.
We closed it for the sake of war!
Forgive us Lord we did not please.
To open Babell in time of peace.

Bobi Roberts

[1] Sunday School   [2] Narrow Path   [3] Debts

St Clement's, Rhayader

On Love

Man cannot live
without love. He remains a being
that is incomprehensible to himself if love
is not revealed to him. His life is senseless if he
does not encounter love, if he does not experience it
and make it his own, if he does not participate intimately
in it. This is why Christ the Redeemer 'fully reveals man to
himself'. The man who wishes to understand himself
thoroughly – and not just in accordance with partial, often
superficial, standards and measures of his being – he must
with his unrest, uncertainty and even his weakness and
sinfulness, with his life and death, draw near to Christ.
How precious must man be in the eyes of the Creator,
if he 'gained so great a Redeemer,' and if God
'gave his only Son' in order that man
'should not perish but have
eternal life.'

Pope John Paul II

So it was that
I learned that love was
our Lord's meaning. And I saw
for certain, both here and elsewhere,
that before ever he made us, God loved
us; and that his love has never slackened,
nor ever shall. In this love all his works have
been done, and in this love he has made
everything serve us; and in this love our life is
everlasting. Our beginning was when we
were made, but the 'love in which he
made us never had beginning. In it
we have our beginning. All this we
shall see in God for ever.
May Jesus grant this.
Amen.'

Mother Julian of Norwich

Holy Trinity (Old Parish Church), Llandrindod Wells

Whosoever thou art
that enterest this
church, leave
it not without
one prayer to
God for thyself,
for those who
minister, and for
those who worship here.

St Mary's, Gladestry

This wonderful hymn, sung to the tune of Calon Lân, has particular meaning I think, when one knows that it was sung during the great Welsh Revival of 1904 by the miners coming up from their shifts, and one can surely imagine it reverberating round the valleys.

Dyma gariad fel y moroedd,
Tosturiaethau fel y lli:
Twysog bywyd pur yn marw
Marw i brynu'n bywyd ni.
Pwy all beidio â chofio amdano?
Pwy all beidio a thraethu'i glod?
Dyma gariad nad a'n angof
Tra fo nefoedd wen yn bod.

Here is love, vast as the ocean,
Loving-kindness as the flood;
When the Prince of Life my ransom,
Shed for me His precious blood.
Who His love will not remember?
Who can cease to sing His praise?
He shall never be forgotten,
Through heav'n's everlasting days.

Ar Galfaria yr ymrwygodd
Holl ffynhonnau'r dyfnder mawr;
Torrodd holl argaeau'r nefoedd
Oedd yn gyfain hyd yn awr:
Gras a chariad megis dilyw
Yn ymdywallt yma 'nghyd,
A chyfiawnder pur a heddwch
Yn cusanu euog fyd.

On the mount of crucifixion,
Fountains opened deep and wide,
Through the flood-gates of God's mercy
Flowed the vast and gracious tide;
Grace and love like mighty rivers
Poured incessant from above,
And heav'n's peace and perfect justice
Kissed a guilty world in love.

Gad im dderbyn Dy holl gariad,
A Dy garu, ddyddiau'n bod;
Gad im ddyfal geisio'r Deyrnas
Gyda'm mywyd i Ti'n glod.
Ti yn unig yw'r gogoniant,
Nid oes arall welaf sydd,
Ti sy'n puro a sancteiddio,
Ti Dy Hun a'm gwnaeth yn rhydd.

Let me all Thy love accepting,
Love Thee, ever all my days;
Let me seek Thy kingdom only
And my life be to Thy praise;
Thou alone shalt be my glory,
Nothing in the world I see;
Thou has cleansed and sanctified me,
Thou Thyself hast set me free.

Y n Dy wir y caf fy arwain
Gan Dy ysbryd trwy Dy lef;
Mae dy ras yn llanw f' angen,
Trwy gael ffydd yng ngrym y nef.
Dy holl lawnder sy'n ymdywallt
Trwy Dy gariad ynof fi,
Yn ddi-fesur llawn, di-derfyn
Wrth im ildio'r oll i Ti.

In Thy truth Thou dost direct me
By Thy Spirit through Thy Word;
And Thy grace my need is meeting,
As I trust in Thee, my Lord.
All Thy fullness Thou art pouring
In Thy love and power in me,
Without measure, full and boundless
As I yield myself to Thee.

Gwilym Hiraethog 1802–1883

St Garmon's, St Harmon

St David's, Heyope

At the Time of Shearing

Heavenly Father, the creator of all shepherds
and those they care for in the green pastures
of life, we thank you ... for the skill in their
hands, as they prepare their flocks for the
summer of life . . . and for the sheep, as
they provide for the comforts of
mankind. Give us O Father, the desire
and strength to be good stewards of Your
creatures, for You have promised to care for
man and beast in Your loving kindness. This
humble prayer we ask through the Good Shepherd
Himself, our Lord and Saviour Jesus Christ.

The Venerable Wynford Rees

At the Time of Harvest

Heavenly Father, we come in thanksgiving
for the harvest that we have been able to
reap yet once again on our journey in
life. You have provided for our
labours on the farm, in the garden
or wherever the challenge is to be
found. Even in moments of
despair, when nature was beyond
our understanding, You did not
desert us. We thank You for
bestowing Your gifts so richly for the
needs of ourselves and those of mankind
through Jesus Christ our Saviour.

The Venerable Wynford Rees

All Saints, Newbridge-on-Wye

God's 'Amazing Grace'

Amazing grace – how sweet the sound –
  that saved a wretch like me!
    I once was lost, but now am found,
      was blind, but now can see.

      'Twas grace that taught my heart to fear,
        and grace my fears relieved;
        how precious did that grace appear
        the hour I first believed.

      Through many dangers, toils and snares,
      I have already come;
     'tis grace hath brought me safe thus far,
      and grace will lead me home.

      When we've been there ten thousand years
      bright shining as the sun,
       we've no less days to sing God's praise
        than when we've first begun.

John Newton 1725–1807

He giveth me more grace when burdens grow greater,
He sendeth more strength when the labours increase;
To added afflictions He addeth His mercies,
To multiplied trials His multiplied peace.

When we have exhausted our store of endurance,
When our strength has failed ere the day is half done,
When we reach the end of our hoarded resources,
Our Father's full giving is only begun.

His love has no limit, His grace has no measure,
His power no boundary known unto men;
For out of His infinite riches in Jesus
He giveth and giveth and giveth again.

Author unknown

      My Grace is Sufficient for You.
      2 Corinthians 12:9

St Padarn's, Llanbadarn Fawr

Builth Wells Male Voice Choir

A Love Song

You ARE beautiful,
but it has nothing to do with you.
You are beautiful because you are in Me.
I know!
We both see the you that makes you hide in shame,
but it is no matter to Me.
It's you who seeks to maim.
I see you beautiful;
in you My Plan fulfilled.
I see you changing.
In you My Heart is thrilled.
I have chosen you. Do you not see?
I don't make mistakes.
Your life is here in Me.
I know you are distracted now
whilst upon the earth.
You sin. You take your eyes off Me,
yet still I see your worth
and I repeat, 'You are beautiful.'
And your repentant tears melt My Heart
to a tidal wave of love.
You cannot know yet how much I love you,
how much I want you,
but know I gave My Life that you might do so.
Not because of the you *you* know,
but because of the you *I* know.
And I call you beautiful.

Suzie Hunt

I have caused thee to multiply as the bud of the field,
and thou hast increased and waxen great,
and thou art come to excellent ornaments:
thy breasts are fashioned, and thine hair is grown,
whereas thou wast naked and bare.
Ezekiel 16:7

St Cewydd's, Aberedw

The River Wye   Afon Wy

(A river states in her own
language that God has
planned the journey).

It was born on Plunlimon
when God created the
world. Llangurig was
its cradle.

A lovely valley was
blessed to see it grow.

Reference to Irfon
and Ithon as veins.
Sounds of fords like
a nice melody.

It smiled on the Wernos
near Erwood where
Hywel Harris and
Williams Williams
were discussing religion.

As it enters England
near Glasbury it is
looking more sad,
but she carried the
drovers to Hereford
or Ross.

The Wye is near Monmouth
and has aged near Chepstow
and it ends its life in
the Bristol Channel,
although it's not
so peaceful!

But the kind Creator
is sure to take her
back to Plunlimon
to start again
for future
generations to
see its beauty.

Bobi Roberts

(Dywed afon yn ei hiaith Mae efe sy'n
trefnu'r daith) (Elfed)

Ar ben Plunlimon draw y ganed
Afon Gwy pan greodd Duw y byd,
Llangurig oedd ei chrud.
A Dyffryn hyfryd gafodd fraint
O'i gweld yn tyfu'n fawr ei maint.

Gwythenau'r Ithon ddaw,
A llaf'r Irfon dlws
I godi nerth eu gwerth
Wrth riniog llawer drws.
Daw sain rhaeadrau hyfryd hon
Fel alaw ber i lonni'r fron.

Fe ganodd llawer yn eu tro,
A'th sain yn sisial ger y Gro,
Ymwelwyr oedd y rhain i gyd,
A Mabon ysbrydolai' bryd.
O dan y Bont ymlusgaist draw,
A weithiau'n flin ar ôl y glaw.

Fe welaist tithau'r galar
Ger Aberedw drist,
Pan laddwyd ein Llwy Olaf
A rhoi ei ben mewn cist.
A'i gludo gan y bradwyr cudd
I Lundain draw i dderbyn budd!

Fe wenaist ar y Wernos
Lle bu'r caniedydd pêr
Mewn seiat gyda Hywel
Yng ngolau'r hyfryd sêr.
A gwenu wnaeth dy donnau mân
Ger Errwd pan y clywaist di ei gân.

Mor dawel wyt yn llifo
I wastad Lloegr brudd
A gorlif Llyn Syfaddan
Ar Llynfi'n gwrido'th rudd
Ac o Rhyd Spens, sydd ar y ffin
Y Porthmyn gludaist trwy bob hin.

Fel 'rwyt ti yn heneiddio
Ymlusgo wnei yn llefn
I Henffordd, ac i Fynwy doi
I Gymru'n ôl drachefn,
Yn Sianel Bryste mae dy fedd,
Er nad yw hwnnw'n hyfryd hedd!

Ond, mae'r Creawdwr tyner
Yn siwr o'th gludo di
Yn ôl i ben Plunlimon
I gychwyn arall li;
A llonni cenedlaethau ddaw
A'th holl hyfrydwch di ben draw.

St Mary's, Llanfaredd

Nature

O Lord my God
when I in awesome wonder,
consider all the works
Thy hand has made,
I see the stars
I hear the rolling thunder
thy pow'r throughout
the universe displayed.

Then sings my soul
my Saviour God to Thee:
how great Thou art,
how great Thou art.
Then sings my soul,
my Saviour God, to Thee:
how great Thou art,
how great Thou art.

When through the woods
and forest glades I wander,
and hear the birds
sing sweetly in the trees;
when I look down
from lofty mountain grandeur,
and hear the brook,
and feel the gentle breeze.

And when I think that God,
his Son not sparing,
sent him to die,
I scarce can take it in
that on the cross,
my burden gladly bearing,
he bled and died
to take away my sin.

When Christ shall come
with shout of acclamation
and take me home –
what joy shall fill my heart!
Then shall I bow
in humble adoration
and there proclaim,
my God, how great Thou art!

Russian hymn translated by Stuart K. Hine, 1953

Seasons of Life

Springtime follows winter, and each summer leads to fall.
The pattern of the seasons flow, and answer to God's call.
Around us in His garden, the flowers bloom and fade,
To sleep throughout the winter, in each meadow, wood and glade.
Some only stay a season, so briefly we can share,
Their colour and their beauty, their soft perfume of the air.
God give us all our season, the sunshine and the rain.
He knows our joy arid sadness, He shares with us our pain.
Let Him take your hand in autumn, feel the joy that His words bring,
For when we reach the peace of winter we shall wake up in the spring.

Humfrey Temple, 1991

The Lord is my strength and shield;
my heart trusted in Him and I am helped.
Psalm 28:7

St Padarn's, Llanbadarn Fynydd

The Heart of Wales

The radiant hills of Radnor glow amongst the ancient barrows
A welcome to its cultured home in its absorbent meadows.
While quiet churches lie in wait like shepherds in the shadows.

Moel Hywel, Moelfre and Wilym bald around Llanbadarn Fynydd,
A true community intact leading to the Dolydd.
While Penybont is Trotting Trade 'tween Vron and fair Moelynwydd.

The rivers greet you with a smile, the Elan, Ithon, Marley,
As they weave down towards the Wye, just like a loving family;
While Nantmel greets with gratitude that hosts the roots of Sophie.[1]

From Offa's Dyke, towards the heart of Wales from Border Counties:
Knighton, Norton and Presteigne guards all its rural beauties.
While Radnor Old and New await their guests from o'er the bound'ries.

Maesllwch, Baskerville, and Rhydspens who cared for all the Drovers
In days gone by; they found their food and drinks dispensed, and shelter;
Shaded by the Rhulen Hill, Bryn Gwyn, Rhosgoch, Llanbedr.

The Lakes! They also welcome all tucked in around the garnedd.[2]
That helps our folk to show their skills, our culture and etifedd[3]
The real Croeso witnessed by the thousands in Llanelwedd.

Bobi Roberts

The pastures are clothed with flocks:
and the little hills rejoice on every side:
they shout for joy, they also sing.
Psalm 65:12–13

---

[1] Rhys Jones   [2] Cairn   [3] Heritage

St Michael's, Bryngwyn

God's Friend

When God had made the earth and sky,
The flowers and the trees,
He then made all the animals
And all the birds and bees.

And when the work was finished
Not one was quite the same;
He said 'I'll walk this earth of
mine
And give each one a name'.

And so He travelled Earth and
Sea,
And everywhere He went
A little creature followed Him
Until its strength was spent.

When all were named upon the Earth
And in the Sky and Sea
The little creature said 'Dear Lord
There's not one left for me'.

The Father smiled, and softly said
'I've left you to the end,
I've turned my own name back to front
And called you DOG – my friend'.

Sent from Canada. Author unknown.

Who shall separate us from the love of Christ? . . .
For I am persuaded, that neither death nor life, nor angels,
nor principalities, nor powers, nor things present,
nor things to come, nor height, nor depth, nor any other creature,
shall be able to separate us from the love of God,
which is in Christ Jesus our Lord.
Romans 8:35, 38 and 39

St Bride's, Cwmdauddwr

God is Love

You see, Fynn, people can only
love outside and can only kiss
outside, but Mister God can
love you right inside, and Mister
God can kiss you right inside,
so it's different. Mister God
ain't like us; we are a little bit
like Mister God but not much yet
. . . You see, Fynn, Mister
God is different from us because
he can finish things and we can't.
I can't finish loving you because
I shall be dead millions of
years before I can finish,
but Mister God can finish
loving you, and so it's not
the same kind of love is it?

From 'Mister God, This is Anna' by Fynn

Love is glad when you are glad,
is sad when you are sad,
is hurt when you are.
Love is never so wrapped
in himself that he can't listen
to you, and hear you.
Love accepts you exactly
as you are – is happy for your
strengths and is sorry for you
in your weakness, however
unacceptable it might appear.
Stands beside you in your struggle.
Love knows no time and is always available.
Love may criticise what you
do but never you, and looks
with you for the right path for you.
Love makes no judgments and has
a deep respect for you; love shares
his all with you: his time his possessions, his talents.
Love grows by sharing himself; love drives out fear;
love is eternal and never dies; Love cares.

Author unknown

St Teilo's, Llandeilo Graban

Prophecy for Wales

Several people have been given a prophecy recently
that the 'wells' of mid Wales must be unblocked;
and that is where revival is going to begin.
This poem came to Chris Daniels in August 1998,
and he has kindly given me permission to use it.

Unblock the well my people
Won't you unblock the well?
Let my Kingdom come
Let my will be done
Unblock the well.

The river poured through in 1904
But it disappeared underground.
Could it happen again like it happened before?
Can't you hear my thunder sound?

*Your sons and your daughters
shall prophesy, your old men
shall dream dreams, your
young men shall see visions.*
Joel 2:28

And water will flow once more from the throne
When my rain falls again on this land;
Are the culverts repaired, are the wells overgrown?
This time will my people stand?

And the river of life will flow again,
And heaven will cast out hell;
Jesus your Lord once again will reign,
So you must unblock the well.

Gracious Father, let all Your people in Wales be ever
mindful of the importance of what is happening in
our midst. Let us not be like the foolish virgins
who let their oil run out, so that when the hour
came they were not prepared.

Loving Father, keep us always alert so that
when the time comes for You to call upon
us, we shall be able to answer with alacrity
'Yes, Lord we are ready.' We ask this in
Jesus' precious Name.

Amen.

St Michael's, Cascob

Part II

The Second Grace
At the Time of Fellowship

In a moment of silence, let it be our care and delight to
thank Almighty God for the blessings of life –
particularly on this day . . .

for the glory of creation in the world around us;
in our Principality, and especially in our Shire
County of Radnor . . .

for the blessings we enjoy in our work on the land,
and in the nurture of God's creatures . . .

for the joy in this Festival of work and pleasure,
and for our fellowship, laughter and compassion.

And now O Father, we ask for Your blessing on those
around this table, upon the food we eat and on all those
less fortunate than ourselves.

Amen

The Venerable Wynford Rees

This section comprises some Thoughts on Living,
with a particular emphasis on not rushing around,
which seems to be one of the scourges of modem day life.

St Mary's, Bettws Disserth

Risk

To laugh is to risk appearing the fool
 To weep is to risk appearing sentimental
  To reach out for another is to risk involvement
   To expose feelings is to risk exposing our true self
    To place our ideas, our dreams before the crowd is to
    risk loss
     To love is to risk not being loved in return
     To live is to risk dying
     To hope is to risk failure
    But risk we must,
   Because the greatest hazard in life is to risk nothing
  The man, the woman who risks nothing, is nothing.

Reality

The greatest of all
life's adventures
is the quest to become real.

This is not achieved
by the pursuit
or the winning
of pleasure,
 power and possessions.

 It is essentially
 the discovery
 of the divine depths
 within ourselves.

  We the redeemed
  have been given life
  for one reason only,
   to be loved and to love.

George R. Leonard

Taliesin and the Alternatives

As
 the three
 drops of rain
  fell on his
  finger Taliesin
 sang: 'Gwion no
 longer, all time runs
 in me now, like a
 river, downward to a
 sea that carries in its
 sunless womb the
 tides of all men's
 striving for the truth,
 setting a seal on all
 our life-long ills,
 and leaving us no
  alternatives
 but death or
  birth.

*From the 'Book of Broceliande'
by John Matthews*

47

St David's, Colva

Leading a Good Life

Not how did he die?
But how did he live?
Not what did he gain?
But what did he give?
These are the units to measure the worth
Of this man as a man, regardless of birth.
Not what was his station?
But had he a heart?
How did he play His God-given part?
Was he at hand with a word of good cheer
To bring back a smile or banish his fear?
Not what was his church or what was his creed?
But had he befriended those really in need?
Not how did the formal obituary run?
But how many grieved when his life's work was done?

Anonymous

You are a child of God. Your playing small does not
serve the world. There's nothing enlightened about
shrinking so that other people won't feel secure around
you. We were born to make manifest the glory of
God, that is within us. It's not just in some of us; it's in
everyone. And as we let our light shine we unconsciously
give light to other people to do the same. As we are
liberated from our fear our presence automatically liberates
others.

Marianne Williamson
(quoted by Nelson Mandela in his inaugural speech).

God chose the foolish things of the world to shame the wise;
God chose the weak things of the world to shame the strong . . .
It is because of Him that you are in Christ Jesus
who has become for us wisdom from God.
Part of 1 Corinthians 10:25–28

St Mary's, Newchurch

Values

Looking back to my childhood of bygone days,
I wanted protection and I longed for praise.
I wanted treasures that were far out of reach.
I longed for love – only giving can teach.
Now I look back nearly ninety years.
And I know that throughout my hopes and fears
A Master of Light was there for me
To show my life's values and what they should be
The 'I' and the 'Ego' must vanish from sight
So that love and compassion can capture the light.
Giving from God to all those who seek
Strengthens the strong, and protects the weak.
To love and to give God's gifts to man
This we must do to fulfil His plan.
To give and to live so the world becomes whole
This is God's Mission for every soul.

Cecilia Rogers

We Promise to Serve

A Guest is the most important visitor to our premises.
He is not dependent on us, we are dependent on him.
He is not an interruption of our work, he is the purpose of it.
He is not an outsider in our business, he is part of it.
We are not doing him a favour by serving him, he is
doing us a favour by giving us an opportunity to do so.

Mahatma Gandhi

These things I command you, that ye love one another.
John 15:17

St Michael's, Llanfihangel Nant Melan

We Are Responsible for Our Own Destiny

Why are murder, pillage and arson
And rape allowed by the Deity?
I will write to the Times, deriding our parson,
Because my God has afflicted me.

We had a kettle: we let it leak:
Our not repairing it made it worse.
We haven't had any tea for a week . . .
The bottom is out of the Universe!

This was none of the good Lord's pleasure,
For the Spirit He breathed in Man is free;
But what comes after is measure for measure
And not a God that afflicteth thee.

As was the sowing so the reaping
Is now and evermore shall be.
Thou art delivered to thine own keeping.
Only Thyself hath afflicted thee!

Rudyard Kipling

Isn't it strange that princes and kings,
And clowns that caper in sawdust rings,
And ordinary folk like you and me
Are builders for eternity?
And each is given a bag of tools;
An hour-glass and a book of rules,
And each must build e'er his time has flown
A stumbling-block or a stepping-stone.

Author unknown

*Ye have not chosen Me, but I have chosen you,
and ordained you that ye should go and bring forth fruit.*
John 15:16

St Peter's, Llanbedr Painscastle

B Cheerful

B Cheerful, **B** Grateful,
B Hopeful, **B** Firm,
B Peaceful, **B**enevolent,
Wishing to Learn

B Courageous, **B** Gentle,
B Liberal, **B** Just,
B Aspiring, **B** Humble,
(Because Thou Art Dust)

B Penitent, Circumspect,
Sound in the Faith,
B Active, Devoted,
B Faithful to Death

B Honest, **B** Humorous,
Forgiving and Dear,
B Dependent, **B** Love Like,
And You'll be Secure

B But Half as Perfect,
As these lines suggest,
And here and hereafter
thou'st surely be blest.

Selected by Marcia Pearson-Gregory

Take my yoke upon you, and learn of me.
Matthew 11:29

St Mary's, New Radnor

'If' for a Christian

If you can stand before false accusations,
  And lift your head in grace and face the lies;

If you can join in another's celebrations,
  While life falls in ruin before your eyes.

If you can grieve with others who are grieving,
  Yet find in Christ a peace beyond all griefs;

If you can love those who are unbelieving,
  and yet stand firm and sure on your beliefs;

If you can lose all wealth and worldly treasure,
  And count it as the loss of so much dust;

If you can scorn success by mortal measure,
  Striving only for rewards that cannot rust;

If you can put your hand to Christian labour,
  Be buried with Christ, your sins all put to end;

If every day you can love your neighbour,
  You will receive the crown of life, my friend.

Look at James 1:2–12 for encouragement and guidance.

Blessed is the man that endureth temptation:
for when he is tried, he shall receive the crown of life,
which the Lord hath promised to them that love Him.
James 1:12

St Michael's, Llanfihangel Helygen

Slow Me Down, Lord

Slow me down, Lord.
Ease the pounding of my heart by the quieting of my mind.
Give me, amid the confusion of the day, the calmness of the everlasting hills.
Break the tension of my nerves and muscles with the soothing music of the singing streams that live in my memory.
Help me to know the magical, restoring power of sleep.
Teach me the art of taking miniature vacations, of slowing down to look at a flower, to chat with a friend, to pat a dog, to read a few lines from a good book.
Slow me down, Lord, and inspire me to send my roots deep down into the soil of life's enduring values, that I may grow toward the stars of my greater destiny.

Cardinal Cushing, 1979.

Mary hath chosen that good part,
which shall not be taken away from her.
Luke 10:41

It is time to cry out with all our hearts to God:
'Teach me your ways that I may walk with you and find favour with you.' It is tragically possible to know the Word of God like the Pharisees, but to be totally out of touch with its author, the Word made flesh who dwells in the hearts of those who are lowly in spirit and who seek His face. What will you choose? The barrenness of busyness or the fruitfulness of a Mary who chose to sit at His feet?

Author Unknown

St Cynllo's, Llangunllo

Take Time to See

It seems so hard to understand
As I look out across the land
That all I view belongs to me,
I ought to take more time to see!

The distant hills and mountains high,
The rolling clouds and bright blue sky,
No one can take these views from me
As long as I have eyes to see.

A timid deer with haunting look
Who stands refreshed by yonder brook
Knows not that he belongs to me,
Oh, what a thrilling sight to see!

The song of birds so gay and clear
That fill the morning air with cheer
And fragrant flowers of every hue
That stand erect bedecked with dew,

All these and more belong to me
If I but use my eyes to see.
When evening shadows gather nigh
And twinkling stars light up the sky.

I hear my Master say to me
'I made it all for you to see.'
My heart grows warm with faith and pride
To know that He is by my side.

Author unknown.

Wait on the Lord, and He shall save thee.
Proverbs 20:22

St Cynllo's, Llanbister (winter)

St Cynllo's, Llanbister (summer)

Listening to the Voice of God

I thought this would be a very easy matter, and so I began to get still. But I had no sooner commenced than a perfect pandemonium of voices reached my ears, a thousand clamouring notes from without and within, until I could hear nothing but their noise and din. Some of them were my own voice, some of them were my own questions, some of them were my prayers. Others were the suggestions of the tempter, and the voices of the world's turmoil. Never before did there seem so many things to be done, to be said, to be thought; and in every direction I was pushed and pulled, and greeted with noisy acclamations of unspeakable unrest. It seemed necessary for me to listen to some of them, but God said, 'Be still, and know that I am God.' Then came the conflict of thoughts for the morrow, and its duties and cares; but God said, 'Be still'. And as I listened, and slowly learned to obey, and shut my ears to every sound, I found, after a while, that when the other voices ceased, or I ceased to hear them, there was a still, small voice in the depths of my being that began to speak with an inexpressible tenderness, power and comfort. As I listened, it became to me the voice of prayer, and the voice of wisdom, and the voice of duty, and I did not need to think so hard, or pray so hard, or trust so hard, but that 'still, small voice' of the Holy Spirit in my heart was God's prayer in my secret soul, was God's answer to all my questions, was God's life and strength for soul and body, and became the substance of all knowledge, and all prayer, and all blessing; for it was the living God himself as my life and my all.

This is our spirit's deepest need. It is thus that we learn to know God; it is thus that we receive spiritual refreshment and nutriment. It is thus that our heart is nourished and fed; it is thus that we receive the Living Bread; it is thus that our very bodies are healed, and our spirit drinks in the life of our risen Lord, and we go forth to life's conflicts and duties like the flower that has drunk in, through the shades of night, the cool and crystal drops of dew. But, as the dew never falls on a stormy night, so the dews of his grace never come to the restless soul.

We cannot go through life strong and fresh on constant express trains; but we must have quiet hours, secret places of the Most High, times of waiting upon the Lord when we renew our strength, and learn to mount up on wings as eagles, and then come back to run and not be weary, and to walk and not faint.

Author unknown

Be still and know that I am God.
Psalm 46:10

Holy Trinity, Llandrindod Wells

Growing Older is Part of God's Plan

You can't hold back the dawn
or stop the tides from flowing
Or keep a rose from withering
or still a wind that's lowing.
And time cannot be halted
in its swift and endless flight
For age is sure to follow youth
like day comes after night . . .
For He set our span of years
and watches from above
Replaces youth and beauty
with PEACE and TRUTH and LOVE.
And then our souls are privileged
to see a hidden treasure
That in youth escaped our eyes
in our pursuit of pleasure . . .
So Birthdays are but blessings
that open up the way
To the everlasting beauty
of God's eternal day.

But the path of the just is as the shining light,
that shineth more and more unto the perfect day.
Proverbs 4:18

St David's, Rhulen

One Day at a Time

The past is history
The future is a mystery
but today is a gift
which is why it is called the present.

Sufficient unto the day is the evil thereof.
Matthew 6:34

Take Time

Take time to think –
It is the source of power.
Take time to play –
It is the secret of perpetual youth.

Take time to read –
It is the fountain of wisdom.

There is
always music
amongst the trees
in the garden but
our hearts must be
very quiet to
hear it.

Take time to pray –
It is the greatest power on earth.

Take time to love and be loved –
It is a God-given privilege.
Take time to be friendly.
It is the road to happiness.

Take time to laugh –
It is the music of the soul.
Take time to give –
It is too short a day to be selfish.

Take time to work –
It is the price of success.
Take time to do charity –
It is the key to Heaven.

In your patience possess ye your souls.
Luke 21:9

All Saints, Glasbury-on-Wye

Evil

The Collect for the First Sunday in Advent.

Almighty God, give us grace to cast away the works of darkness,
and put upon us the armour of light, now in the time of this mortal life,
in which Thy Son Jesus Christ came to visit us in great humility;
that, on the last day, when He shall come again in His glorious
majesty to judge both the quick and the dead, we may rise to the
life immortal; through Him, who liveth and reigneth with Thee in
the unity of the Holy Spirit, one God, now and for ever.

Amen.

Let us walk in the light of the Lord.
Isaiah 2:5

If only there were evil people somewhere insidiously committing evil deeds,
and it was necessary only to separate that from the rest of us and destroy
them. But the line dividing of good and evil cuts through the heart of every
human being, and who is willing to destroy a piece of his own heart?

From the Gulag Archipelago by Alexander Solzhenitsyn

The very powers of darkness are paralysed by fear.

Oswald Chambers

St Mary's, Pilleth

A Proclamation for God's Protection

No weapon that is formed against us shall prosper and every tongue
which rises against us in judgment we do condemn. This is our
heritage as servants of the Lord and our righteousness is from
You, O Lord of hosts. If there are those who have been
speaking or praying against us, or seeking harm or evil to
us, or who have rejected us, we forgive them. Having
forgiven them, we bless them in the name
of the Lord.

Now, we declare, O Lord, that You and You
alone are our God, and besides You there is no
other – a just God, and a Saviour, the Father,
the Son and the Spirit – and we worship You.

We submit ourselves afresh to You tonight in
reserved obedience. Having submitted to you,
Lord, we do as Your Word directs. We resist the
devil; all his pressures, his attacks, his
deceptions, every instrument or agent he would
seek to use against us. We do not submit! We resist
him; drive him from us and exclude him from us in
the Name of Jesus. Specifically we reject and repel:
Infirmity, pain, infection, inflammation, malignancies,
allergies, viruses, and every form of witchcraft.

Finally, Lord, we thank You that through the sacrifice of Jesus
on the cross, we have passed out from under the curse and entered
into the blessing of Abraham whom You blessed in all things:
Exaltation, health, reproductiveness, prosperity, victory, and God's favour.

Derek Prince Ministries

*Because your adversary the devil, as a roaring lion,
walketh about, seeking whom he may devour.*
1 Peter 5:8

St Anno's, Llananno

Against the Night

When men have lost all reason and evil seems to win,
Then compromise is treason and silence is a sin.
Let all who hate the darkness prepare to stand and fight;
The children of the morning must stand against the night.

When all that wisdom treasures is treated with disgrace,
And idols of damnation are set up in their place.
When every holy symbol is fading out of sight,
The children of the morning must stand against the night.

We'll do the work of heaven against a setting sun,
Until the final darkness when no work can be done.
Then watching for the Bridegroom with oil lamps burning bright,
We will worship in the darkness and stand against the night.

Against that final darkness no human strength can stand;
The evil shall be shattered but not by human hand.
The maker of the morning will come in Holy Light
That burns in righteous anger and wrath against the night.

Then comes the final morning when all will be restored,
The shadowlands transformed by the glory of the Lord.
When every darkened memory is washed in healing Light
Where there will be no warfare, for there will be no night.

Clay McLean

The tares are the children of the wicked one;
the enemy that sowed them is the devil.
Matthew 13:38–39

St Edward's, Knighton

The End of the Century

In a high-speed world please teach us to walk,
In a world of computers, please teach us to talk,
In a pre-packaged world, teach us how to create,
In a violent world, teach us how not to hate.

But, please, above all, let us never forget,
To open our minds and acknowledge our debt
To You, our Creator, and Jesus, your Son:
May Thy Kingdom come and may Thy Will be done.

Geoffrey Culverwell, 1999

Oh my
good and merciful
Father now on the last day
of the departing year and the
last day of the departing century I
desire to thank Thee for blessings that
Thou hast showered upon me all my
life. Thy bountiful providence of all
needful for myself, my partner and all our
dear children and above all for the blessed
hope I have of spending my Eternity
where I shall see my Holy Redeemer
worshipped by Angels. Oh may I join
in the praises to my Jesus who
bought my pardon by His precious
Blood on the Cross. Oh my
Father for his sake blot
out all my sins.
Amen

Thomas Watkins
from 'The Diary of a Countryman', 1900

St Michael's, Discoed

PART III

THE BIBLE AND PRAYER

The Third Grace

Grant, Lord, your blessing on
our meat that all the strength
from what we eat may serve
your holy Will. Grant that our
sharing in this meal may make
more true the love we feel for
you and for our friends. Grant
that our pleasure may remind us
of the needs of all mankind for
food and knowing you.

Amen

*A Grace written by the late Right Reverend J. Poole-Hughes,
Bishop of Llandaff. Selected by the late Venerable Elwyn John,
Archdeacon of Brecon.*

We perish if we cease from prayer;
O grant us how to pray;
and, when to meet Thee we prepare;
Lord, meet us by the way.

James Montgomery (1771–1854)

St Bridget's, Llansantffraed-in-Elwell

THE FOLLOWING IS A LITTLE SECTION ON PRAYER AND ITS IMPORTANCE

All the Difference

I got up early one morning and rushed right into the day;
I had so much to accomplish that I didn't have time to pray.

Problems just tumbled about me, and heavier came each task.
Why doesn't God help me? I wondered. He answered: 'You didn't ask.'

I wanted to see joy and beauty, but the day toiled on grey and bleak,
I wondered why God didn't show me. He said: 'But you didn't seek.'

I tried to come into God's presence; I used all my keys at the lock.
God gently and lovingly chided, 'My child, you didn't knock.'

I woke up early this morning, and paused before entering the day,
I had so much to accomplish that I had to take time to pray.

*Eye hath not seen, nor ear heard, neither have
entered into the heart of man, the things which God
hath prepared for them that love Him. But God hath
revealed them unto us by His spirit.*
I Corinthians 2:9–10

Six requisites for prayer: faith, submission, sincerity,
perseverance, forgiveness and the name of Jesus.

Cast your bread upon the waters and it will come back buttered.

St Mary's, Abbeycwmhir

The Power of Prayer

Although we are led
in prayer by our Vicar in our Church
services, we must never be afraid to speak to Our Lord
in our everyday lives as individuals. Whatever time of day or
night, especially lying in bed awake, we can communicate with
Our Lord and Saviour. He is approachable, understanding and gentle.
He always listens. There are many elements in prayer, but, in the same
way we are led in Church, our words must include praise for Him, asking
forgiveness for our sins and weaknesses, followed by the specific requests
we bring to Him and ending with grateful thanks for His bountiful
goodness. He is there all the time and His Holy Spirit works true
wonders if only we take the time to ask in humility. Whether
busy or lonely, our lives are altered by approaching Our
Lord, so let us never seek excuses to forget Him
as we go about our daily lives.

Robin Gibson-Watt

Prayer Being Answered

*For as the rain cometh down, and the snow from heaven and returneth
not thither, but watereth the earth, and maketh it bring forth and bud,
that it may give seed to the sower, and bread to the eater,' So shall My
word be that goeth forth out of My mouth; it shall not return unto me
void, but it shall accomplish that which I please.*
Isaiah 55:8–9

A Thought on God's Word

If an earthly king . . . wrote you a letter, would you not read
it with joy? The King of heaven has sent a letter to you . . .
yet you almost despise such a gift, so priceless a treasure.
When you read the Gospel, our Lord is speaking to you.
And while you read you are talking to Him.

Tikhon of Zadonsk

St Llyr's, Llanyre

Some Things about The Bible

All that I have ever taught of art, everything that I have written, whatever greatness there has been in any thoughts of mine, whatever I have done in my life, has simply been due to the fact that, when I was a child, my Mother daily read with me a part of the Bible, and daily made me learn a part of it by heart.

John Ruskin

Queen Victoria, (when asked the secret of Britain's greatness replied):
'The Bible, the greatest possession we have.'

To the Queen at her Coronation:
'We present you with this Bible, the most valuable thing this world affords. Here is wisdom. This is Royal Law. These are the lively oracles of God.'

Sin keeps you from the Bible.
The Bible keeps you from sin.
Sin separates you from the Bible.
So read the Bible.

A Prayer Before Reading the Bible

We open ourselves to the WISDOM of the Word of God.
We open ourselves to the GUIDING of the Word of God.
We open ourselves to the POWER of the Word of God.

Father, You spoke Your Word and the earth was birthed,
Speak new life to us this day;
Jesus, You came to us as the Word of God,
Speak new life to us this day;
Spirit, you awaken us to the Word of God,
Speak new life to us this day.
Father, Son and Holy Spirit,
Welcome us now to the word of Life.

St Michael's, Llanfihangel Rhydithon

Two Wonderful Prayers to Be Said Each Morning

O, Holy Spirit of God, visit now this soul of mine,
and tarry within it until eventide.
Inspire all my thoughts.
Pervade all my imaginations.
Suggest all my decisions.
Lodge in my will's most inward citadel, and order all my doings.
Be with me in my silence and in my speech,
in my haste and in my leisure,
in company and in solitude;
in the freshness of the morning
and the weariness of the evening,
and give me grace at all times to rejoice in
Thy mysterious companionship.

John Bailey from 'A Diary of Private Prayer', 1936

The Armour of God

Lord, be with us now as we begin a new day.
Protect me with the armour you have made available to me.
Lord, I put on the belt of truth surrounding and protecting my body,
The breastplate of righteousness so enveloping my heart.
I will carry a shield of faith,
protecting me at all times from the devil's arrows.
Upon my head I place now, Lord, a helmet of salvation,
And your Word will become my sword.
I pray Lord for your help and guidance and protection for this day;
Fill me with your Holy Spirit, and teach me your ways in all I do and say.
I stand firm in your love;
And your power will enable me to resist the enemy's attacks.
Thank you Lord.

From the Harnhill Centre.
See Ephesians 6: 10–18.

St Mary's, Kinnerton

The 'End' of Prayer

Never
say you
will pray
about a thing:
(just get on and)
pray about it. Our
Lord's teaching about
prayer is so amazingly
simple but at the same time
so amazingly profound that
we are apt to miss His meaning.
The danger is to water down what
Jesus says about prayer and make
it mean more common sense; if it were
only common sense, it was not worth
His while to say it. The things Jesus says
about prayer are supernatural revelations.

*For your Father knoweth what things
ye have need of, before you ask Him,*
Matthew 6:8

If God sees that my spiritual life will be furthered
by giving the things for which I ask, then He
will give them, but that is not the end
of prayer. The end of prayer is that I come
to know God Himself. If I allow my
bodily needs to get out of relationship
to God, then those needs will keep
me morbidly interested in myself
all the time, much to the
devil's enjoyment. We have to
leave ourselves resolutely
in God's hands and
launch out into the
work of intercession
on the basis of
faith in the
perfect
redemption
of Jesus.

Oswald Chambers Daily Devotional Bible

St David's, Llanddewi Ystradenni

Two Children's Prayers

Morning Prayer

The morning comes with shining light;
My God took care of me last night.
I wish I could be good all day
And put all naughty thoughts away.
I do love God who is so good;
He gives me warmth and clothes and food.
He always hears me when I pray,
He knows all that I do or say.
So when the morning light I see,
I think of all His love for me.

Evening Prayer

Dear Jesus, will You listen
To tiny little me.
And make me good and gentle
As I should like to be.

I am so weak and little
And never can do right,
Unless You help me, Jesus,
With all Your loving might.

Selected by Marjorie Gibson-Watt

But Jesus called them unto Him, and said,
Suffer little children to come unto me, and forbid them not:
for of such is the Kingdom of God.
Luke 18:16

St David's, Glascwm

Noon Prayer

Lord, give us a vision for our country. May it be a land of
justice and peace, where people do not take unfair advantage
of each other; where all have sufficient, and poverty and
vice will have no place to fester; where seeking to serve
others means more than honour and success; where
order does not rest on force; where faith, hope
and love flourish and all work for the
Will of God. In the Name of
Jesus Christ.

I will bring them to the place I have chosen as a dwelling for my name.
Nehemiah 1:9

The Crosswinds Prayer for Britain

Lord God of heaven, you are great and we stand in awe of you.
You faithfully keep your New Covenant with those people who trust
in you and in Jesus Christ, whom you have sent.

Look down on us Lord, and hear our prayers as we pray for your
Church here in this nation. We confess that we, your people, have
sinned. We and all the people of this nation have gone away from
you and your Gospel, the Good News about Jesus Christ.

Remember now what you have done in Him and not what we
deserve. For His sake renew and restore your people, rebuild your
Church and win this nation for Christ and His Gospel once again.

We ask this in His name and for your honour and glory . . .
Amen
Based on Nehemiah 1:5–11

St Michael's, Michaelchurch-on-Arrow

A Saints and Angels Prayer

St Michael of the flaming sword:
Arm me;

St Francis of the creatures:
Calm me;

St Christopher of the travellers:
Guide me;

St David of the hills:
Be beside me;

St Antony of the lost:
Find me;

St Martin of the cloak:
Unwind me;

Gabriel of the eager wings:
Fire me;

Christ, with Your angels come,
Come, Inspire me.

Jennifer Holland

Sing unto the Lord, O ye saints of His, and give thanks at the
remembrance of His holiness.
Psalm 30:4

St Peter's, Evancoyd

Forgiveness

The hatred which divides nation from nation,
race from race, class from class,
Father forgive.

The covetous desires of men and nations
to possess what is not their own,
Father forgive.

The greed which exploits the labours of men,
and lays waste the earth,
Father forgive.

Our envy of the welfare and happiness of others,
Father forgive.

Our indifference to the plight
of the homeless and the refugee,
Father forgive.

The lust which uses for ignoble ends
the bodies of men and women,
Father forgive.

The pride which leads to trust in
ourselves and not in God,
Father forgive.

Coventry Cathedral Prayer

Everyone thinks that forgiveness is a great idea
until they come to practise it themselves.

With apologies to C. S. Lewis

*Forbearing one another, and forgiving one another, if any man have
a quarrel against any: even as Christ forgave you, so also do ye.*
Colossians 3:13

Nantgwyllt Church, Cwmdauddwr

Help Me, O Lord

Help me, O Lord, to descend
into the depths of my being,
below my conscious and
subconscious life
until I discover
my real self, that
which is given
me from You,
the divine
likeness in
which I am
made and into
which I am to
grow. The place
where Your
spirit communes
with mine, the
spring from which
all my life rises.

Hallowed be Thy name,
not mine,

Thy Kingdom come,
not mine,

Give us peace with Thee,
peace with men,

Peace with ourselves,
and free us from all fear.

Dag Hammarskjöld

George Appleton

Thou takest the pen – and the lines dance.
Thou takest the flute – and the notes shimmer.
Thou takest the brush – and the colours sing.
So all things have meaning and beauty in that space beyond time
where thou art. How, then, can I hold back anything from Thee?

Dag Hammarskjöld

St Michael's, Cefnllys (summer)

St Michael's, Cefnllys (winter)

Girls, into Your Hands . . . !

Dear
graduates!
For six years
we have striven
with might and main to
convey to you the spirit and
bearing of the true woman of
the, Christian West. Now you are
called upon to defend that spirit against
a purely materialistic view of life. You will
enjoy being at last on your own and
independent, but you will soon also realise that it is
not so easy to withstand all the temptations of
freedom or to find people who think as you do. Most
young people today live at a huge distance from things of the
spirit: they value too highly what gives them raw pleasure, like
eating, drinking, smoking, playing, television. It is your task to raise on
high the spiritual values in life and absorb them into your lives: the
language of the poets, noble music, art, wise words of the thinkers,
or meaningful books . . .

May God grant you to keep the Faith and to have the strength
to resist the spirit of the age, to swim against the current
and as Christian mothers, be it physical or
by spiritual motherhood, to rescue our sinking
world. For that purpose I wish you all
the blessing of God, the Mother of
God's protection, and the
intercession of our
patron, St. Theresa
of the Child
Jesus.

St Theresien Gymnasium, St Vinzenzstr, D 53809 Schonenberg, West Germany

*Farewell speech to girls finishing at St Theresien Gymnasium,
SSPX secondary school for girls in Western Germany, given in the
summer of 1997 by Sister Michaela, headmistress.*

St Meilig's, Llowes

O Dad

O Dad trugarog a graslawn
cofia am dy bobl sydd yn
cadw a gwarchod y tir. Bydd
yn gymorth iddynt mewn
cyfyngder ac arwain hwy y
llwybr at oleuni.

Amen

O merciful and gracious Father,
do not forsake your people
who look after the land.
Help them in their tribulations
and lead them on the path
towards light.

Amen

Ein Tad yr hwn wyt yn y
nefoedd Cofia am dy
deulu ar y llawr a
chynorthwyo nhw i weld
dy ogoniant di mewn
natur ar dy ddaear.
Bendithia bawb sydd yn
gwarchod dy ogoniant di.

Amen

Our Father in Heaven,
remember your family
on earth and help
them to see your
splendour in nature.
Bless all those who are
custodians of your glory.

Amen

Beryl Vaughan

*No man, having put his hand to the plough,
and looking back, is fit for the Kingdom of God.*
Luke 9:62

Holy Trinity, Chapel-of-Ease, Bettws Clyro (above)
St Michael's and All Angels, Clyro (below)

Teach Us, O Lord

Teach us, O Lord to attempt great things for Thee,
and from Thee to expect great things,
that we may be strong to win men
to love and serve Thee,
for the Honour and Glory of Thy great Name;
through Jesus Christ our Lord.

William Carey

*William Carey was known to be very persistent;
when asked the secret of his success, he replied:
'I can plod; I can persevere in any definite pursuit.
To this I owe everything.'*
*William worked tirelessly to make God's truth known in every
aspect of Indian society. He translated the Bible into the local
languages, and developed an extensive library system. He
published the first Indian-language newspaper, and with his
concern for God's creation brought conservation efforts and
reform in agricultural practices. Seeing no area of his life as
outside of God's concern, William demonstrated what one man
can do to disciple an entire nation in God's ways.*

Because we cannot be clever and honest
and are inventors of things more
intricate than the snowflake
Lord have mercy.

Because we are full of pride in our humility,
and because we believe in our disbelief
Lord have mercy.

R. S. Thomas

Socrates taught us: know thyself.

St David's, Howey

Part IV

Death, Suffering, Healing and Light – Always Light

The Fourth Grace

Creator God, source of all goodness and growth
you give seed for us to sow, and bread for us to eat,
you encourage us to work together
in fellowship and service for the good of all;
Give us grateful hearts for what we have received
and a loving concern for the needs of others
that the whole world may give you thanks and praise.

Amen

The Right Reverend the Bishop of Swansea and Brecon

Who is Jesus?

He comes to us as one unknown without a name as of old.
By the lakeside He came to those men who knew Him not.
He speaks to us the same word: 'Follow thou me!'
and sets us to the tasks which He has to fulfil for our time.
He commands, and to those who obey Him,
whether they be wise or simple,
He will reveal Himself in the toils, the conflicts, the sufferings
which they shall pass through in His fellowship,
and, as an ineffable mystery, they shall learn
in their own experience who He is.

Albert Schweitzer

St Steffan's lychgate, Llanstephan

Guidance

I said to the
man who stood
at the Gate of
the Year, 'Give me
a light that I may
tread safely into the
unknown'. And he replied,
'Go out into the darkness and
put your hand into the hand of
God. That shall be to you better than
light and safer than a known way.' May
that almighty hand guide and uphold us all.

Minnie Haskins 1875–1957

*This prayer was quoted by King George VI in his
Christmas day broadcast on 25 December 1939,
and is now pinned up outside George VI's tomb/chapel at Windsor.*

Suffering and Healing

How poor are they that have no patience!
What wound did ever heal but by degrees?

Iago from 'Othello', William Shakespeare

Bear ye one another's burdens, and so fulfil the law of Christ.
Galatians 6:2

God whispers to us in our pleasures, speaks in our conscience,
but shouts in our pain: it is his megaphone to rouse a deaf world.

C. S. Lewis, 'The Problem of Pain'.

Prayer For Healing

Keep us O Father in the light and warmth of Your presence.
Let Your healing hands soothe the pain of those who suffer.
Support those who are weak,
and encourage those in the depth of despair.
Enable us O Lord, in Your divine compassion,
to face the morrow with hope and joy.
This we ask through Jesus who healed and restored in Your name.

Amen

The daffodils are paid for by the January snow.
Without the shadow of suffering we would not know the light of joy.

I will extol You, O Lord, for You have lifted me up,
And have not let my foes rejoice over me. O Lord my God,
I cried out to You and You healed me.
Psalm 30:1–2

St Cewydd's, Disserth

Death

Death is not the extinguishing of the light
but the blowing out of the candle because the dawn has come.

Rabindranath Tagore 1861–1941

The Ship

I stand upon a seashore,
a ship spreads her white sails to the morning
breeze, and heads across the blue ocean. She is an
object of beauty and strength, and I stand and watch her
until at length she hangs like a speck of white cloud on the horizon
just where the sea and the sky meet to mingle with each other.
At my side someone says 'There! she's gone.' Gone where? Gone from
my sight – that is all. She is just as large in mast and spar and hull as
when we sailed close by, and just as able to bear her living freight
to the place of destination. Her diminished size is in my vision
alone. At the moment when someone says 'There she's
gone,' other eyes are watching her coming and other
voices take up the shout, 'Here she comes!'
And that is dying.

Bishop Brent

Blessed are you, Lord our
God, lover of souls: you uphold us
in life and sustain us in death: to you be glory
and praise for ever! For the darkness of this age is
passing away as Christ the bright and morning star brings to
his saints the light of life. As you give light to those in
darkness who walk in the shadow of death, so remember in
your kingdom your faithful servants that death may be for
them the gate to life and to unending fellowship with
you; where with your saints you live and reign,
one in the perfect union of love now
and for ever. Amen

*Written by David Stancliffe, late Bishop of Salisbury,
for the commemoration of the dead.*

St David's, Cregina

Courage

You can shed tears that she is gone
or you can smile because she has lived.

You can close your eyes and pray that she'll come back
or you can open your eyes and see all she's left.

Your heart can be empty because you can't see her
or you can be full of the love you shared.

You can turn your back on tomorrow and live yesterday
or you can be happy for tomorrow because of yesterday.

You can remember her and only that she's gone
or you can cherish her memory and let it live on.

You can cry and close your mind,
be empty and turn your back or you can do what she'd want:
smile, open your eyes, love and go on.

David Harkin

Encouragement

The life that I have is
all that I have,
And the life that I have is yours.
The love that I have
of the life that I have
Is yours and yours and yours.

A sleep I shall have,
a rest I shall have,
Yet death will be but a pause,
For the peace of my years
in the long green grass
Will be yours and yours and yours.

Leo Marks

*But seek ye first the Kingdom of God,
and His righteousness;
and all these things
shall be added unto you.*
Matthew 6:33

St David's, Llanddewi Fach

A Hymn for The Eucharist

To your table   I draw near,
yet not worthy   to be here.
You invite me   to take rest,
you the host   and I the guest.

Is it possible   to meet,
sit with you   to drink and eat?
May we touch   and taste you, Lord
in the bread and   wine outpoured?

Open my closed   mind to see
how such costly   gifts are free.
Give my clouded   eyes fresh sight
of the world   seen in your light.

Feed   mind
and   body,
heart   and soul
bread   and wine
to   make
them   whole.
At   your
table   we
will   kneel,
that   our
broke'   ness
may   heal.

Amen

Do this in remembrance of Me.
I Corinthians 11:24

St Matthew's, Llanelwedd interior

A Consolation

When in disgrace with fortune and men's eyes
I all alone beweep my outcast state,
And trouble deaf heaven with my bootless cries,
And look upon myself, and curse my fate,
Wishing me like to one more rich in hope,
Featured like him, like him with friends possest,
Desiring this man's art, and that man's scope,
With what I most enjoy contented least;
Yet in these thoughts myself almost despising,
Happy I think on thee – and then my state,
Like to the lark at break of day arising
From sullen earth, sings hymns at heaven's gate;
For thy sweet love remembered, such wealth brings,
That then I scorn to change my state with kings.

William Shakespeare.

It is better to light a candle than to curse the darkness.

Chinese proverb

For Light

Lord grant me,
I pray Thee in the name of
Jesus Christ the Son, my God,
that love which knows no fall
so that my lamp may feel Thy kindling touch,
and know no quenching;
may burn for me
and for others may give light.

Prayer of Columbanus

St David's, Whitton

Casserole de Marriage

Take a girl
and a man, put them in
a house or a flat. Take all their
love and strain carefully to
remove any trace of sarcasm,
bitterness or irritation. Add two
large measures of good temper,
intelligence, tolerance, patience,
understanding, thoughtfulness and
laughter. Then add half measure of
tidiness; and half measure of
ambition. Add a dash of spice of
discussion, and mix all
ingredients together with their
love and let stand. If too much
spice has been used, the
mixture will curdle. If so
add another measure
of understanding
and tolerance,
and the
mixture
will again become
smooth. Watch carefully –
curdling must never be allowed
to continue overnight. This
will endanger the whole.
Moisten mixture thoroughly
with large quantity of milk
of human kindness, mix
with equal parts of common
sense and laughter. Sprinkle
liberally with a sense of
humour and divide
evenly between two
people. Cook carefully
over the fire of
knowledge, and
love of God, and
let stand for
a long
time.

Recipe for Happiness

One cup of confidence
One cup of love
In a pan of happiness
Mix the above
Add a pinch of tenderness
A tablespoon of trust
Stir well in the sunshine
Roll out a loving crust
Flour with contentment
Keep all free from strife
Fill with understanding
And bake well all your life.

Let every one of you in particular so love his wife as himself.
Ephesians 5:33

St John the Divine, Cwmbach Llechrhyd

Adversity

When things go wrong as they sometimes will
When the road you're trudging seems all uphill,
When funds are low and debts are high,
And instead of a smile you have to sigh.
When care is pressing you down a bit,
Rest in God's love – and never quit.
Life can be strange with its twists and turns
And many a failed man's turned away
When with God's help he'd have won the day.
Don't give up though the pace seems slow
For you may succeed with another go
Success is failure turned inside out.
The silver glint in the cloud of doubt.
You never can tell how close you are
The goal may be near when it seemed so far.
So turn to the Lord when you're hardest hit;
Put your trust in Him – never quit.

Take therefore no thought for the morrow . . .
See Matthew 6:25–34

Lord, help me to remember that nothing is going to happen
to me today that You and I cannot handle together.

Hope

God has not promised skies always blue,
Flower-strewn pathways all our lives through;
God has not promised sun without rain,
Joy without sorrow, peace without pain.
God has not promised we shall not bear
Many a burden, many a care,
He has not told us we shall not know
Toil and temptation, trouble and woe.

But God has promised strength for the day
Rest for the labour, light for the way,
Grace for the trials, help from above,
Unfailing sympathy, undying love.

Rejoicing in hope; patient in tribulation; continuing instant in prayer.
Romans 12:12

. . . for the morrow shall take thought for the things of itself
Matthew 6:34

font   greenstone

St Stephen's, Old Radnor

Night-Time

Dear
God, it seems
so odd calling you
God. It makes you seem so
far away. And yet when I look up
at all the stars in the night sky, I feel
you are out there, looking down on us
all. And when I fall asleep the stars go
on looking down and I know that you,
too, are watching over me. And when I
wake up in the morning you will be there
with the sun. Perhaps the stars are all your
angels watching over us? Perhaps each
star is a guardian angel? Perhaps each
of us has a star as well as a guardian
angel to ourselves? Just as when
Jesus was born he had a star to
himself. Oh, God, let my star
watch over me this night.
Goodnight, God.

James Roose-Evans

St Peter's, Crug-y-Budder

St Michael's, Beguildy

One Life

He was born in a stable,
in an obscure village. He
worked in a carpentry shop
until he was thirty. From
there He travelled less than
two hundred miles. He never
owned a house. He never won an election, He never went to college,
He never owned a home, He never had a lot of money. He had no
credentials but Himself. He became a nomadic preacher. Popular
opinion turned against Him; He was betrayed by a close friend, and
His other friends ran away. He was unjustly condemned to death,
crucified on a cross among thieves on a hill overlooking the town
dump and when dead laid in a borrowed grave. Nineteen centuries
have risen and fallen, and today He is the central figure of the human
race. 'All the armies that ever marched, and all the navies that have
ever sailed, all the parliaments that have ever sat and all the powerful
rulers that have ever reigned have not affected the life of man on
this earth as much as He.
He is the Messiah, the Son
of God, JESUS CHRIST
****

I am the way, the truth and
the life. No man cometh
unto the Father but by Me.
Believe Me that I am in the
Father, and the Father in
Me. Whatsoever you ask in
My name that will I do, that
the Father may be glorified
in the Son. If you love Me,
keep My commandments.
Peace I leave with you, my
peace I give unto you. Let
not your heart be troubled,
neither let it be afraid.

Extracts taken from John 14

St Mark's, Nantmel Ysfa

Faith

But they that wait upon the Lord
shall renew their strength;
they shall mount up with
wings as eagles.
Isaiah 40:31

Never once – since the world began
Has the sun ever stopped shining;
His face very often we could not see
And we grumbled at His inconstancy,
But the clouds were really to blame, not He,
For behind them, He was shining.

Our good Lord said: 'All things will be well;' and
'You will see for yourself that all manner of things will be well.'

From the 'Revelations of Divine Love' by Mother Julian of Norwich.

I have set my rainbow in the clouds,
and it will be the sign of the covenant
between me and the earth.
Genesis 9:13

St Cynog's, Boughrood

The Fruit of The Spirit

Love

Joy

Peace

Longsuffering

Kindness

Goodness

Faithfulness

Gentleness

Self control

Galatians 5:22–23

Ye shall know them by their fruit
Matthew 7:16

St. Andrew's, Presteigne

Tapestry

Almighty God who dost fashion what is lovely through the work of our hands: weave the threads of our lives into the wholesome tapestry of our community, where we may praise thee for Thy goodness and serve one another for Thy sake.

The Right Reverend E. J. K Roberts

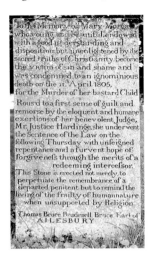

I am only a spark; make me a fire.
I am only a string; make me a lyre.
I am only a drop; make me a fountain.
I am only an ant hill; make me a mountain.
So that I can love and serve you better.
There is not a place where God is not,
wherever I go, there God is.
Now and always he upholds me with his power
and keeps me safe in his love.

See Psalm 139

For there is not a word in my tongue but, lo,
O Lord, thou knowest it altogether.
Psalm 139:5

St Andrew's, Norton

Thanksgiving

We thank thee O Lord our Lord, for our being,
our life, our gift of reason, for our nurture,
our preservation and guidance, for our education,
civil rights and religious privileges, for thy gifts of grace,
of nature, of this world, for our redemption, regeneration
and instruction in the Christian faith, for our calling,
recalling and our manifold renewed recallings,
for thy forbearance and long suffering.
Thy prolonged forbearance many a time and many a year.
For all the benefits we have received, and all the
undertakings wherein we have prospered, for any good we
may have done, for the use of the blessing of this life,
for thy promise and our hope of the enjoyment of good
things to come, for good and honest parents,
gentle teachers, benefactors ever to be remembered,
congenial companions, intelligent hearers, sincere friends,
faithful servants, for all who have profited us by their
writings, sermons, conversations, prayers, examples,
reproofs, injuries. For all these, and also for all other
mercies known and unknown, open and secret,
remembered by us or now forgotten, kindnesses received
by us willingly, or even against our will.
We praise thee, we bless thee, we thank thee and will
praise and bless and thank thee all the days of our life.

O go your way into His gates with thanksgiving,
and into His courts with praise; be thankful unto Him,
and speak good of His Name.
Psalm 100:3

St Mary Magdalene, Bleddfa

When Earth's Last Picture is Painted

When earth's last picture is painted and the tubes are twisted and dried,
When the oldest colours have faded, and the youngest critic has died,
We shall rest, and, faith we shall need it – lie down for an aeon or two,
Till the Master of All Good Workmen shall put us to work anew.

And those that were good shall be happy: they shall sit in a golden chair;
They shall splash at a ten-league canvas with brushes of comets' hair.
They shall find real saints to draw from – Magdalene, Peter and Paul;
They shall work for an age at a sitting and never be tired at all!

And only the Master shall praise us, and only the Master shall blame;
And no-one shall work for money, and no-one shall work for fame,
But each for the joy of the working, and each, in his separate star,
Shall draw the Thing as he sees It for the God of Things as They are!

Rudyard Kipling

Go ye into all the world, and preach the Gospel to every creature.
Mark 16:15

LIST OF ILLUSTRATIONS

Penelope Bourdillon

Penelope Bourdillon lived for over forty years with her husband at Llwyn Madoc, Beulah, near Llanwrtyd Wells, which has been in their family for generations. They brought up their four children in that idyllic setting, and then moved to a smaller house on the estate in 2002. It gives her enormous pleasure to see her son, Patrick, and his wife living there now with their three teenage daughters.

Having spent every summer holiday in Scotland, where her brother still runs a much-loved family estate with great interest and knowledge, Penelope has always been surrounded by people who are connected with land management and the care of the countryside. Mervyn, her late husband, was closely involved with forestry for many years, and he and Penelope had a particular involvement with the Brecknock Young Farmers, and a special affinity with their local club, Beulah. Mervyn was president of Beulah Show for forty-nine years, and Penelope was delighted when she was asked to take on that role when he died.

The love she has for horses and dogs gives ready precedence to her love of people and, in a spiritual context, she continues in her endeavours through learning and witness. Her restlessness in the quest to share her spiritual experience through her efforts to see these beautiful country churches alive in worship is so evident to those who know her.

MARCIA GIBSON-WATT

Marcia Gibson-Watt was married in 1971, since when she settled and lived with her husband Robin and their four children at Gelligarn, Llanyre, Llandrindod Wells.

As a trained graphic designer she worked with Laura Ashley and has since travelled widely in Asia and Europe – attracting a profound respect for her skill as an artist. While her home has provided a local exhibition for the many who have enjoyed her hospitality, the Royal Academy has housed her work, as have various galleries in London and the provinces. In 1989 Marcia was commissioned to paint a scene of judging in the main ring at the Royal Smithfield Show involving the Queen Mother making the presentation to the owner of the prize-winning animal. It was the exhibition of her miniatures of churches in Powys at Bleddfa in 1988 that inspired her for what has been achieved in this book.

Marcia's spiritual life has long been exercised in the service of the Church. As a past member of the governing body of the Church in Wales she was able, in her gentle but forthright manner, to bear witness to her commitment to her faith. To this end she continues to seek a greater understanding of the faith and to proclaim it through her skill. For Marcia, these churches are not mere buildings but sanctuaries which have been hallowed by the prayers and worship of countless Christians throughout the ages.